Let Freedom Ring

Let Freedom Ring

Introduction By Walter Anderson

And Justice for All: Under the dome of the Jefferson Memorial. Photo by Susan L. Steele of Washington, D.C.

1992

The Continuum Publishing Company
370 Lexington Avenue
New York, N.Y. 10017

Copyright © 1992 by Parade Publications, Inc.

Design by Ira Yoffe

Printed in Hong Kong

Library of Congress Cataloging-in-Publication Data

Let Freedom Ring: a pictorial celebration / by the winners of the
Parade-Kodak National Photo Contest: introduction by Walter Anderson
        p.   cm.
            ISBN 0-8264-0613-0
        1. Photography, Artistic
        2. Liberty – Pictorial works.
        I. Eastman Kodak Company.
        II. Parade (New York, N.Y.)
            TR654.L455 1992

779'.9973928 – dc20   92-13607 CIP

Any
Resemblance...
Is Purely
Coincidental:
Portrait by
Alan and Kim
Meeks of
Cottonwood, Calif.

Amber Waves: The whole world seems to celebrate along with cousins Anna Leet (left) and Alexandra Law, both 3. Photo by Alexandra's mother, Wendi Wavrin Law of Omaha, Neb.

T his book is a remarkable tribute to the imagination, verve and creativity of America's everyday photographers—ordinary folks who take extraordinary pictures. When Parade Magazine and Eastman-Kodak announced they were sponsoring a National Photo Contest entitled "Let Freedom Ring" to observe the 200th anniversary of the Bill of Rights, some people might have raised their eyebrows. After all, though the first ten Amendments of the U.S. Constitution may serve as the bedrock of our liberties, how do you honor them in photographs? Can you depict in pictures such ideals as freedom of speech, religion and the press, security against unreasonable searches and seizures, the right to trial by jury—in short, the philosophical concept of liberty itself?

The answer, given by the nearly quarter of a million people from every state of the Union who entered pictures in the competition, is "Darn right you can." As the Editor of Parade, which has a circulation of more than 36 million across the country, I never doubted the outcome. The response to our magazine reaffirms every week our readers' awareness of their heritage, their interest in the news and the personalities of the day, and their alertness to challenge, whether posed by a provocative article or by a stimulating competition. Our distinguished judges—Eddie Adams, Pulitzer Prize-winning photographer; Dr. Joyce Brothers, psychologist; Warren E. Burger, retired Chief Justice of the United States; Alex Haley, author of *Roots* and other books, and Sally Jessy Raphael, talk-show hostess—all reported being struck by the sheer variety and ingenuity of these pictorial interpretations of what is, after all, a concept embodied in a political document written 200 years ago.

As a matter of fact, judging by the amazing scope of the entries that poured in right from the first week of the contest, the Bill of Rights is anything but an abstract or remote ideal to the people of this country. That's why you'll find in this book, which contains the winning entries, pictures not only of a patriotic or commemorative nature, but pictures devoted to the daily lives of friends, relatives and neighbors, and to the many events, activities and occurrences we enjoy as part of daily existence in this free land. Freedom, these pictures tell us, includes along with the flags, statues and parades, such basic American rituals as prayer and picnics, marriage and graduation, music and baseball.

One other aspect of the contest I'd like to comment upon is the sheer beauty of so many of the winning pictures. Subject matter aside, the brilliance and balance of the photographs *per se* deeply impressed the judges, as a well as officials of Eastman-Kodak, our co-sponsors. The National Photo Contest is open to professional and amateur photographers alike, but at least as far as the quality of the entries is concerned, the line of demarcation between the two groups grows increasingly undistinguishable.

There are those of us still alive who can remember the days of the box camera, and the way amateur photographers used to try to pose family members in just the right grouping under just the right light. Today's photographers know how to handle sophisticated camera equipment with an ease and confidence that literally opens up new vistas. And along with their technical skill has grown a new artistic sensibility and creativity.

Best of all, picture-taking has never lost its fun. That explains why you'll find in this book photographs of such zest and originality—pictures that have an important message and deliver it with uncommon grace and artistry. We're proud to present this pictorial anthology of the free lives we all share.

In February, as this book was being put together and as he and the other judges were writing the essays that appear in it, Alex Haley died. In all the years to come, whenever any person aspires to document the history of this nation — in pictures or in words — no account will ever be complete complete without reference to or the inclusion of his extraordinary history of the black experience in America — *Roots*. This book is dedicated to his memory.

Daddy's Home!
Richard Ruffert, 28,
holds his daughter,
Ashley, 3, for
the first time since
he left to serve in
the Persian Gulf.
Photo by his wife,
Sherri Ruffert of
Mount Vernon, Ind.

9

Youngest Patriot? Danielle Benham, 18 months, struck this pose "spontaneously, without any help from adults," says the photographer, Matthew G. Muise of Marblehead, Mass.

Amendment I

Congress shall make no law respecting an establishment of religion, or prohibiting the free exercise thereof; or abridging the freedom of speech, or of the press, or the right of the people peaceably to assemble, and to petition the Government for redress of grievances.

Amendment II

A well regulated Militia, being necessary to the security of a free State, the right of the people to keep and bear Arms, shall not be infringed.

Amendment III

No Soldier shall, in time of peace be quartered in any house, without the consent of the Owner, nor in time of war, but in a manner to be prescribed by law.

Amendment IV

The right of the people to be secure in their persons, houses, papers and effects, against unreasonable searches and seizures, shall not be violated, and no Warrants shall issue, but upon probable cause, supported by Oath or affirmation, and particularly describing the place to be searched, and the persons or things to be seized.

One Nation, Under God: Photo of Irene Ream, 93, by Lois I. Stethem of Niles, Mich.

"O Beautiful for Spacious Skies": The eagle spread its wings, and Barb Gross of Bismarck, N.D., was ready—
capturing, she says,"the shot of a lifetime."

The Sight of Might: "These military planes let me know this country has the power to keep us free," says the photographer, John C. Jones of Sherwood, Ark.

One Marine welcomes another to
Charlie Company in Camp Pendleton,
Calif. Photo by Mrs. Gay Sports, a
schoolteacher in San Diego.

Echoes of 1776: In support of our
Declaration of Independence, the words
of the nation's founders still ring clear:
"We mutually pledge to each other our
Lives, our Fortunes, and our sacred
Honor." Photo by Evelyn Daboll of the
Village of Noank, Town of Groton, Conn.

A Late Afternoon in Dallas: Photo by Teresa A. Turko of Garland, Tex

The Children Speak: Construction on the fence of an elementary school in North Merrick, N.Y., during the Persian Gulf war. Photo by Eileen Moynahan of Garden City, N.Y.

Freedom and Equality—For Everybody: The arms belong to (from left) Raymond Davis, Enrique Atkinson and the Rev. Rachel Wilken, all of Corpus Christi, Tex. Photo by Leah Eileen Wilken, Rachel's daughter, of Corpus Christi.

Red, White and Blue: Daniel Nelson of Rapid City, S.D., a college student, took this photo of a girl with stars in her hands during the 50th-anniversary dedication at nearby Mount Rushmore National Memorial.

The Right of the People To Peaceably Assemble: John W. Pyles, commissioner of Monongalia County, W.Va., sings "God Bless America" at a rally of Persian Gulf war supporters. Photo by Greg Gaspar of Morgantown, W.Va.

A Young Love: While posing for this photograph, Aimee Nicole Plunkett, 8, suddenly turned around and kissed the flag. Photo by Shelly M. Zaikis of Oklahoma City. Later, she superimposed a shot of Aimee taken a year earlier.

Reflections on Freedom: Brandon Scott Lingenfelser, 7, sits at the bottom of a circular metal slide. Photo by his mom, Leslie Boatwright Lingenfelser of Blacksburg, Va.

True-Blue Patriot: Tracey Danielle Daniska, 3, gives her front-porch flag a hug on the Fourth of July. Photo by her mother, Brenda Daniska of Piedmont, S.C.

Golden Waves: Kate Alford, 6, in
the light of the Capitol dome in
Washington, D.C. Photo by her father,
Jamie Alford of Midlothian, Va.

Fair and Impartial: The Roman goddess
Justice graces the dome of the town hall
in Exeter, N.H., built in 1855. Photo by
Cera J. Ageieff of New Boston, N.H.

Equal Justice Under Law: Lines and shadows of the U.S. Supreme Court building in Washington, D.C., evoke the grandeur of the ideal of the Court in a photo by Barbara Reed of Dahlgren, Va.

33

Mr. Jefferson and Me: Chloe Briscoe, 6 months, plays near the Thomas Jefferson Memorial in Washington, D.C. Photo by her father, Greg Briscoe of Laurel, Md.

Freedom Above All: It seems even a man of stone reveres the cast-iron statue of Freedom atop our nation's Capitol building. Photo by James D. Mathews of Liverpool, N.Y.

What Price Freedom? "To me, these figures in Washington, D.C., represented all of the hardship that has gone before, and that will continue in order to preserve our freedom," said the photographer, Kevin Rolly of Gibsonia, Pa., of the Peace Monument, dedicated to members of the Navy who died in the Civil War. Grief, sometimes identified as America, holds her covered face against the shoulder of History, and weeps.

Ultimate Freedom: Patty Presnell, 29, of West Palm Beach, Fla., soars like a bird high above a trampoline. Photo by her husband, A. Paige Presnell.

All Cooped Up:
Chickens confined in
close quarters along
Pennsylvania Route
15 caught the eye of
Helen M. Bain of
Fort Lauderdale,
Fla.

41

Where Have All the Flowers Gone?
One rose salutes the 58,183
U.S. military reported killed or missing in
action and now embodied by the Vietnam
Veterans Memorial. Photo by
Marcy Fine of Birmingham, Ala., a
student at the University of North
Carolina in Chapel Hill.

Reflection of History: Eun Lee, 16, of
Largo, Fla., finds a soldier's name on the
Vietnam Veterans Memorial in
Washington, D.C. Photo by Renée M.
Bouchard of Alexandria, Va.

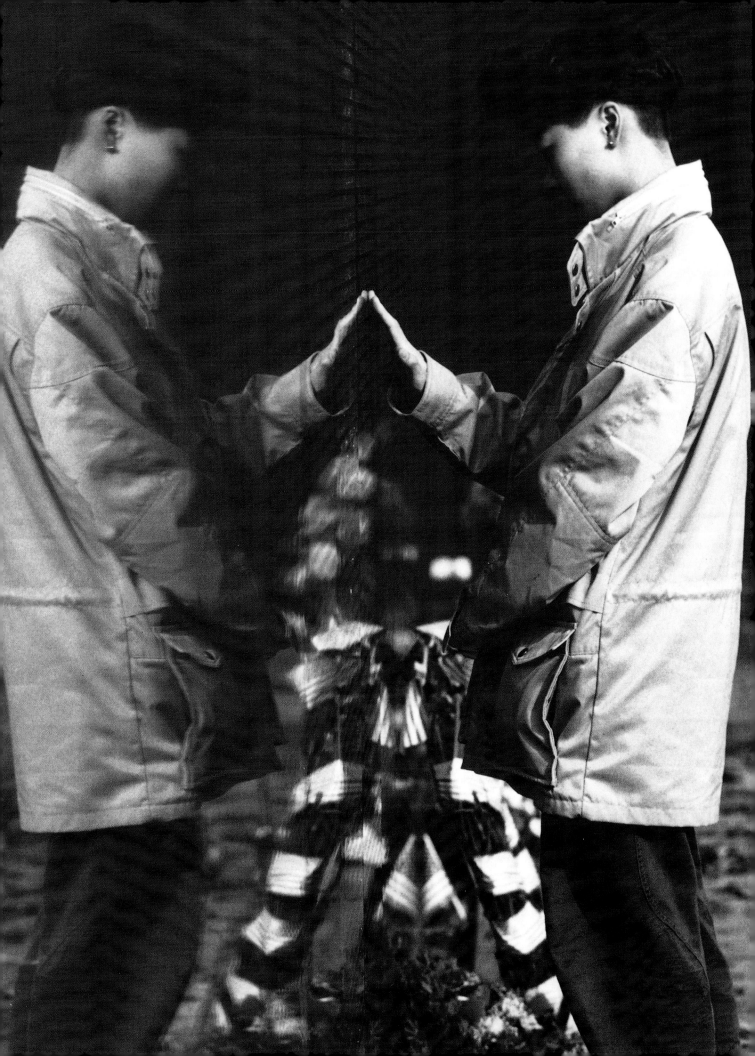

The Price Paid: Photo taken at
Custer Battlefield National Monument in
Montana by Jerry D. Miller of
West Valley City, Utah.

Vestiges of War:
A card tucked
inside one of the
boots reads, "I'm
sorry for not
reaching you in
time." Photo taken
in front of the
Vietnam Veterans
Memorial in
Washington, D.C.,
by Jennifer Smith
of Mountain Home
Air Force Base,
Idaho.

44

... RY E HIMMELREICH · DUANE M NELSON · ERNEST PRESID
FRED R ROBILLARD · RONALD K SCHUKAR · VAN WILLIAMS ·
· JAMES T FAULKNER · EDWARD A MALEWICZ Jr · JIMMIE LEE MINCKS
BERT L WOMACK · NESTOR LORENZO ARGENZIO · WILLIAM R ROMAN
NE W WILLIAMS · JERALD L DOZIER · JOHN M STARKES Jr · ROBERT T EFA
NG · MICHAEL LIPTOCK · DONNY RAY STEVENS · WILLIAM G WHEATLE
· LEROY GARRETT Jr · GARY H JONES · DUANE C SMITH ·
Jr · THEODORE R CHAMBLEY · JUAN BENITEZ · CHARLES R CHEMIS ·
ER · STANLEY E OLMSTEAD · WINFIELD W SISSON · HARLEY B PYLES ·
JEL T BAKER · MANFRED B MILLER · JOHN B WORCESTER · JAMES MASSE
· OWEN T LAVERY · RONALD W MACKLIN · WESLEY McDONIAL
WILLIAM K BARRETT · MICHAEL E DAVIS · JOSEF S HUWYLER
ENDEFER · TIMOTHY J BILKO · JAMES L CRAGAR · RICHARD K JORDAN
MANUEL GONZALEZ-MALDONADA · GEORGE G LUIS · ROBERT J MANN
· MILTON L OLIVE III · THOMAS W PUSSER · MIGUEL BREJO
WARD KEMP · NORMAN A LEIKAM · RICHARD J STES
WILLIAM L MILLER · DONALD C McPHE
N · BEN K McBRIDE · AM R SPATES
JOHN R PETTY Jr · N M LANE · THOM
N · ROBERT E SV · WILLIAM J TEBO
NK OCHOA FL · ARLES W PO

Through My Own Eyes: Michael A. Gerardi Jr. of Albany, N.Y., wanted to capture his own perspective upon seeing the familiar Iwo Jima Memorial in Arlington, Va.

AND MEMORY
MEN OF THE
ES MARINE CORPS
HAVE GIVEN
THEIR COUNTRY
NOVEMBER 1775

Dressed Up for the 50th: The Mount Rushmore National Memorial in South Dakota was formally dedicated on July 3, 1991, which marked its 50th anniversary. Photo by Jan Betten of Spearfish, S.D.

Before the Land Was Ours: Even through America's _un_recorded history,freedom rings. Photo by Doris L. Doerfler of Portland, Ore.

Purple Mountain Majesties: Early morning on Trout Lake in Colorado. Photo by Harold C. Thoma of Florissant, Mo.

This Land Is Your Land: Yellowstone National Park combines the untouched beauty of the elements, flora and fauna.
Photo by Sue Sherman of Enola, Pa.

"I wanted to photograph what I believe is the best symbol of what America means." Photo by Amy C. Tyner of Raleigh, N.C., on a boat cruise in New York Harbor.

In Defense of Peace: Sunset in San Diego, near North Island Naval Air Station. Photo by Dorothy DuBois of Bonita, Calif.

On Freedom's Wings: Fledgling Jennifer Espinoza, 4, gets a lofty sense of liberty. Photo by her mom, Janice Espinoza of Whittier, Calif.

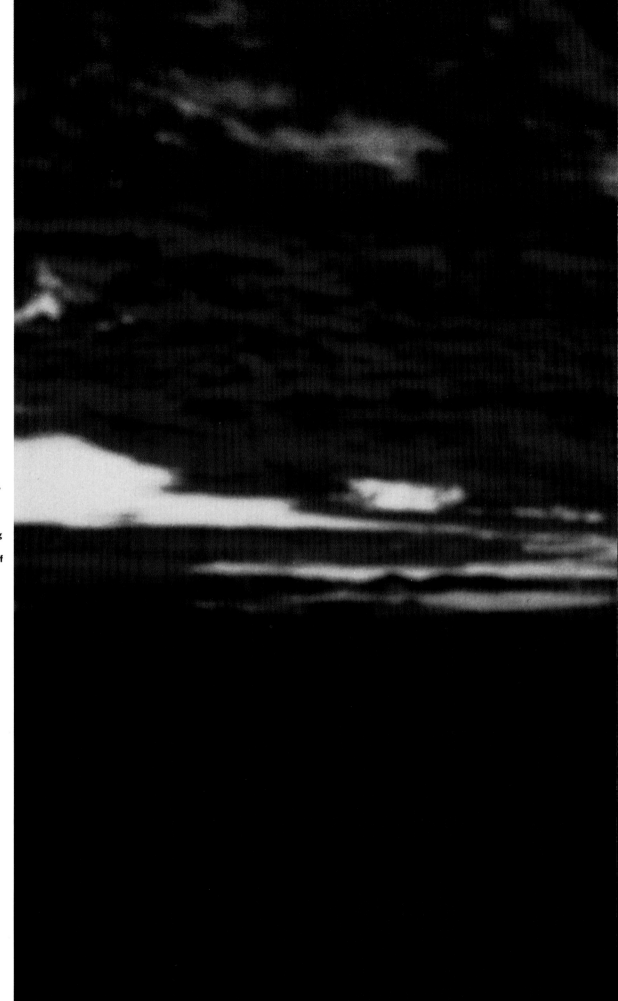

A Ride Home:
Jill Leeson, 2, gets
a lift from Babra
Chirwa under the
radiant night
sky after an evening
hike. Photo by
Ronald P. Symons of
Portland, Ore.

Young Mr. Liberty: Britton B. Banowsky
Jr., 4, holds his torch aloft by the
pool at his home. Photo by his mother,
Cynthia B. Banowsky of Dallas, Tex.

A Perfect Day for Reflections:
The citizens of Park City, Utah, celebrate
"Autumn Aloft" and the pristine
beauty of their town. Photo by Don
Horning of Park City.

Backward View: The Dewey sisters— Evan, 5, and Claire, 2—of Kailua, Hawaii, bask in a breeze. Photo by their mom, Ann Dewey.

The Freedom To Assemble—Upside Down: Thirteen yoga practitioners stand on their heads on the bank of Indian River, Mich. Photo by Elizabeth G. Brauerof Ann Arbor, Mich.

P.E.C. 1991

Hail to the Troops: All the children—ages 5 to 12—at Paul Ecke Central Elementary School in Encinitas, Calif., take a stand in recognition of U.S. troops in the Persian Gulf war last February. Photo by George L. Paul of Encinitas.

Stars and Stripes Forever: Marching as the living flag in the Bristol, R.I., Fourth of July parade were (from left) Andrew St. Ours, Gary Whynot, Ann Mehlmann, Carol Botelho, Carolyn Mott Jaques and Marilyn Mott St. Ours.
Photo by Kathy Brownell of Jamestown, R.I.

71

Ragamuffins on Parade: The drum major on the lead trike is Codey Moyes, 7 months. Photo by Dixie Piper of Sumner, Ill.

This Future Looks Bright: Max McEachern, 11 months, is caught by the sun. Photo by his mother, Alyce C. McEachern of Columbia, S.C.

The Pursuit of Happiness—Animal Style:
Golden Boy takes a cool snooze on a hot
August day, while owner, Loukia George
of Bay Shore, N.Y., snaps the picture.

A Boy's Pursuit of Happiness:
John Robert Andrews, 10, doing what he
loves to do best. Photo by his father,
Robert T. Andrews of Pelham, Ala.

75

Something Old, Something New: Joan and Richard Gaffney wed at Joan's family farm in Bethany, Conn., while her nephews—Mark and Alex Carrington, both 3—and some curious cows look on. Photo by the groom's sister, Susan Gaffney of Westbrook, Conn.

Exercising His Rights: Wayne Augustine takes a break from shopping in Highlands, N.C. Photo by his wife, Valerie Augustine of Gilbert, S.C.

Amendment V

No person shall be held to answer for a capital, or otherwise infamous crime, unless on a presentment or indictment of a Grand Jury, except in cases arising in the land or naval forces, or in the Militia, when in actual service in time of War or public danger; nor shall any person be subject for the same offence to be twice put in jeopardy of life or limb, nor shall be compelled in any criminal case to be a witness against himself, nor be deprived of life, liberty, or property, without due process of law; nor shall private property be taken for public use without just compensation.

Amendment VI

In all criminal prosecutions, the accused shall enjoy the right to a speedy and public trial, by an impartial jury of the State and district wherein the crime shall have been committed; which district shall have previously ascertained by law, and to be informed of the nature and cause of the accusation; to be confronted with the witnesses against him; to have compulsory process of obtaining witnesses in his favor, and to have the assistance of counsel for his defence.

Falling Through Fire: A paratrooper with the 82nd Airborne Division is superimposed against Fourth of July fireworks at the Washington Monument in composite photo by Bill Petros of Washington, D.C.

Ready for Takeoff: Brian J. Keeley, 28,
a fighter pilot now stationed
at Ramstein Air Base in Germany,
snapped this self-portrait in the
cockpit while on duty in Turkey.

Daddy's My Hero:
Lauren West, 3,
with her father, Lt.
Wilk West, at
the Naval Air
Station Oceana in
Virginia Beach, Va.
Photo by
Pamela Trainor of
Virginia Beach.

A Soldier's Hug: Robin Layton Kinsley of Williamsburg, Va., took this picture of Richard Wille, 29, and his daughter, Amanda, 3, in Norfolk.

Homecoming: Corwin Snow, 30, embraces his 3-year-old twin sons, Christopher (left) and Kyle, after returning from a six-month deployment in Japan. Photo by his wife, Kim Snow of Corpus Christi, Tex.

After Desert Storm: The moment of reunion for Sgt. Lee L. Smith and his wife, Esther, snapped by Beth S. Milner of Tampa, Fla.

Lest We Forget: A Civil War re-enactment at Bentonville Battlefield State Historic Site in North Carolina. Photo by Edward Wertz of Hoover, Ala.

"…And the Home of the Brave": Pete Kuld, catcher for the Huntsville (Ala.) Stars, and the umpires pause before a game to observe an American ritual. Photo by Terry Wingo of Madison, Ala.

91

Rookie Excitement: Christine Lindberg, 8, is thrilled about her first Little League Challenger Division season. Pushing her is Cheryl Schroeder, 11. Photo by Christine's mom, Susan R. Lindberg of Coram, N.Y.

Stephen M. Rogers, 3, already is working to be as active as possible. Photo by his teacher, Diane M. Viets of New London, Conn.

A Will To Win: Jim Knaub (left) and Bob Rosenberg pump hard in the Pilgrim Health Care Falmouth (Mass.) Road Race. Photo by Russell F. McKinnon of Alexandria, Va.

Barely Playing: Marina Skiles (left) and her friend Tisha reach for the keys to try a duet for Marina's father Albert Skiles of Fayetteville, Ark., who took the picture.

Indomitable Spirit: John Joseph McGarrity, 6, autistic and born with Down's syndrome, does not talk. "But he loves the piano—the piano is his friend," says Joan Baughman Binford, a registered nurse in Charleston, W.Va., who took this photo.

Flawed but Intact: Ryan Phillips, 4, with mother, Robin, gets to touch the Liberty Bell in a visit to Philadelphia. Photo by Terrence Pattie—also Robin's son—of Fort Worth, Tex. He was 8 at the time.

"Appealing" Discovery: Paul R. Crawford of Prattville, Ala., visited the ranch his great-grandfather had settled in the 1800s in Kendalia, Tex., and found this old train bell.

Still Life for Liberty: A photography class assignment by Brenda B. Machos of Pittsburg, N.H.

On the Hill: Brother and sister Michael and Allison Rushford, show their true colors on a family trip to the nation's capital. Photo by their father, David Rushford of Worcester, Mass.

Spread Your Wings: "The dove represents peace and freedom, the chains represent captivity, and the motion of flying is the movement toward freedom," says the photographer, Jennifer Kerrigan of Annandale, Va.

"The right of the people to be secure...against unreasonable searches and seizures": The Holocaust Memorial in Miami Beach. Photo by Cheryl Levin of Sunrise, Fla

**Want Some News?
Free expression
of fact and opinion is
essential to a
free society. More
than 20 newspaper
dispensers are
backed by
the Federal Trade
Commission in
Washington, D.C.
Photo by Barbara L.
Roche of Studio
City, Calif.**

Freedom To Worship: Father George Gailiusis, 79, of St. Anthony Monastery in Kennebunkport, Maine, reminds us of our debt to the First Amendment. Photo by Michele Doucette of Boston.

"I Made It!" Etop Offiong Udo of Tampa, Fla., snapped a self-portrait to always remember his first day as a U.S. citizen.

Uncle Sam Cries in Denver: Nick Del Calzo, a portrait photographer, caught Donald F. Chambers, 69, off guard—as our Desert Storm victory inspired both joy and sorrow.

Three Friends—One Swing: Posing on the playground at Marshall School in Hempstead, N.Y., are (from left) Ashley Eason, Leslie Chacon and Dominique Merchant, all 5. Photo by Cori Wrobel of Garden City, N.Y.

Rainbow Kids in North Attleboro, Mass.: Friendship is the pot of gold for (from left) Jennifer Haberek, 4, Michael Haberek, 5, Mark Woods, 8, Valerie Woods, 7, Yousuke Yonekura, 4, and Sheldon Frey, 4. Esther C. Deming, also of North Attleboro, says she saw the children and had to take their picture.

Three's Company: Megan Barlow (left) and Amber Bachtel with Holly, a black Labrador retriever. Photo by Ralph Russo of Madison, Wis.

The Joys of Summer: Shawn Whitlock (left), 4, Qiana Sanders (right), 5, and pals pile on their nursery-school aide, Susan Livingston, on a July day in Newark, N.J. Photo by Laura L. Comppen of North Arlington, N.J.

"I Wish": Julia Wilkinson, 7, has high hopes for a great day. Her aunt, Geri M. Tuckett of Philadelphia, Pa., took the photo.

The Blessings of Freedom: Heather Baxter, 9, enjoys the thrills of an amusement-park ride in Williamsburg, Va. Photo by her father, Michael W. Baxter of Edison, N.J.

Sunday Morning in America: First cousins Karl Johnston (left) and Christopher Hankins, both 2, break free of their parents on the way home from church in Springfield, Ill. Photo by Ken Johnston of Indianapolis, Ind.

Big Brother: Anthony Schuck, 5, lends a helping hand to 6-month-old Jordan. Their father, John J. Schuck of Santa Barbara, Calif., snapped the photo.

The Graduate: Bryant O'Neil Davis, 6, of Houston, earns his kindergarten diploma. His dad, Melvin Davis, shot this photo and told us, "I thought, 'This is a perfect example of letting freedom ring through education.'"

He's 100% American: Allen Ray Lamont, 10, of the Oglala Sioux at a gathering of the tribes in Jamestown, Va. Photo by Pamela L. Pouchot of Grafton, Va.

Success Story: Muriel and Joseph Bases of Delray Beach, Fla., celebrate 55 years together. Photo by Gloria Frank of Delray Beach.

Look, Up in the Sky! John D. Dahl, 14 months, flies his first kite with a little help from his grandfather, John M. Dahl, 68, of San Diego. Photo by Sheila K. Ryan, the boy's mother, of Florence, Mass.

Fun on the Farm:
The cow's tail has
just swatted the
rear end of Sharyn
Pasquinelli. The
alert photographer
was her sister,
Deanna L. Mudryof
Pittsburgh, Pa.

For the United Way: Larry Dickens, 27, director of the Pine Belt Boys and Girls Club, with Percy Dewayne Pittman, 7, in an attention-getting photo by Artie Rawls of Hattiesburg, Miss.

To Protect and Defend: Air Force Sgt. Dawn Marie Beener, returning from the Gulf war, hugs her daughter, Ryan, 24 months. Photo by Dawn's mother, Nancy Lee Bailey of Mansfield, Mass.

What It's Really All About: Tiffany Crowther, 8, asks God to bless all she loves. Her mom, Robin Crowther of Bayfield, Colo., took the photo.

Time Out: Emily Whitley, 5, during a summer visit to her new school. Photo by Jeanne S. Fastenau of Greenville, S.C.

Statue of Liberty? Not exactly, but certainly a bold stance taken by Eryka Jade Rice at age 2, at the suggestion of her mother, Deborah. Photo by Eryka's father, Jerry Rice of Florence, Ky.

That's One Happy U.S. Citizen: "The judge 'Americaned' me," said Christopher Stephen Jameson, 2, after his naturalization ceremony. Photo by his mother, Alison Cohn Jameson of Allentown, Pa.

My Son, The Patriot: A proud Steven Goldberg of Acworth, Ga., took this picture of his son, Micah Louis, 4.

Little Miss Liberty: Tasha Weiss Johnson, 5, dons a crown of freedom. Her uncle, Edward Weiss of Takoma Park, Md., took the photo on Independence Day.

Sheriff of Dodge City: Jonathan Ramey gets a bang out of his fourth birthday with a capgun. Photo by his mother, Kimberly Ramey of Pembroke Pines, Fla.

Free as a Bird: Or, rather, a flock of birds. Martha K. Jensen of Honolulu took this photo of her daughter, Meagan K. Snyder, and company.

Amendment VII

In Suits at common law, where the value in controversy shall exceed twenty dollars, the right of trial by jury shall be preserved, and no fact tried by a jury shall be otherwise reexamined in any Court of the United States, than according to the rules of the common law.

Amendment VIII

Excessive bail shall not be required, nor excessive fines imposed, nor cruel and unusual punishments inflicted.

Amendment IX

The enumeration in the Constitution of certain rights shall not be construed to deny or disparage others retained by the people.

Amendment X

The powers not delegated to the United States by the Constitution, nor prohibited by it to the States, are reserved to the States, respectively, or to the people.

Little Miss America:
Caitlin Carlson, 3,
gazes at the Gulf of
Mexico from a piling
on Longboat Key in
Sarasota, Fla. Photo
by her mom, Dawn
Carlson of
Riverview, Fla.

Free-Wheeling Family: Don and Patty Wills of Placerville, Calif., have 25 children (20 adopted). One day, 11 of them took a bike ride up a hill. From left: David, 10; Scott, 9; Janey, 10; Cody, 8; Lucy, 12; Heidi, 9; Bobby, 11; Mark, 13; Aaron, 10; Ryan, 11; and Mindy, 9. Photo by Joanne McCubrey of Placerville.

A s a photographer, I have to look at the technical elements. Is the lighting right, the angle, the background, the colors? Sometimes I wish I didn't have to consider these things. Sometimes when you worry too much about the technical aspects, the subject loses its spontaneity. And the beauty of a photograph is how it makes you feel, what it says to you. If it makes you feel something, then it's good, even if it's a little out of focus and technically bad. I like the spontaneous moment—the moment that tells a story. A portrait or a posed photograph can be very beautiful, but you fool the real people and their feelings when it's actually happening.

People in general consider images important. The evidence is everywhere. How many people do you know who keep a written journal of their vacations? Maybe a few. Now think of how many people you know who chronicle the important events in their lives—weddings, birthdays, special outings—through photography? Just about everyone.

When you pick up a snappy from your trip to Europe five years ago, you can relive the experience. Memories are triggered from that one picture. It will take you back in time. You can recall the time, the place, the event, the person. Like Einstein was to have said, "People change—but a photograph remains the same—you remember people as they once were."

Our society, too, places great importance on images and looks. People buy clothes, cars, jewelry, to look good or to impress others. Consider the advertising industry. The imagery is phenomenal. They use photography, more than anything else, to promote products. They appeal to our senses and desires in the form of images, to sell a product. Flip the pages of any magazine, and what stands out the most, what stops your eye is the photograph.

Photographs are a permanent documentation of history. That's important. People need to know about what's going on, and nothing says it better than pictures.

Photographs act as legal evidence. They can determine guilt or innocence. Photography has no language barrier—it speaks to everybody. A photo can describe an injustice, further a cause. And yet, a photo can be faked. I always hope that every time I squeeze the shutter of my camera and once the photographs are published—that something good will happen to the subjects portrayed—or their cause. And what greater cause than freedom? This was a great contest. The photos were so diverse—really interesting. It's amazing to see how many different images people can relate to one word, one idea. And you can see the correlation. This book is full of good pictures. They all have something to say, whether it's serious or humorous. As long as they touch you, make you think, laugh, cry, they're good pictures.

he Constitution of the United States.
The Bill of Rights. Just saying these words conjures up a sense of authority, a sense of security, the
tenets by which we live our lives. The foundation of our society, of our freedom,
can be found within the pages of these documents. Although we may not think of the Bill of Rights
every day, it is comforting to know that is always there. offering protection and liberty
for each and every American.
At first thought, a photo contest with the Bill of Rights as its theme seemed daunting. But as the photos arrived by the tens of thousands, it became clear that Americans
have many perceptions of what the Bill of Rights means to them, and were able to express their feelings in photographs. This contest also served to refresh our memories as to just what the
Bill of Rights says and how valuable and precious it is.
The range of subject matter in these pictures was astounding, making the selection of just 100 winners quite difficult. The photos that won, however, for all their differences, showed
one thing in common: America at its best.

DR. JOYCE BROTHERS

141

W hat could be a more fitting way
to celebrate the Bicentennial of the Bill of Rights than to have Americans show how—through a
camera—they see freedom in everyday life. The use of a medium that did not exist
200 years ago serves to demonstrate the timeless nature of our basic liberties. As I viewed the
entries, I was moved by the diversity that citizens view our nation and its freedoms. The large
number of excellent entries reinforced my experience that all judging is difficult.
My congratulations not only to the winners, but to all who entered.
On behalf of the Commission on the Bicentennial of the United States Constitution, I thank PARADE
Magazine for the excellent vignettes on the Amendments that they ran throughout the year.
They greatly aided in making this contest part of a "history and civics lesson for all Americans."

RETIRED CHIEF JUSTICE WARREN E. BURGER

If Freedom were a sound, we would hear it as a titanic bass voice – clear and mighty and unaccompanied – from a wide open mouth. Together with tenors, sopranos and altos, Freedom's acoustics would swell of the voices that reverberate off the lofty ceilings of an old, medieval church.

Quite a powerful image, that Freedom. Indeed, can you imagine Freedom sounding tinny? Scratchy? The reason I chose sound to represent my image of Freedom is because sound – or song – is intangible, too, yet so rich and powerful in the way it moves those who listen and guide their lives by it. It gives the listener a reason to feel. Feelings are potent stuff, and have moved many men and women to stand up for their rights, many times, alone.

But that mighty bass voice – an individual – is what makes Freedom so mighty. Freedom is propelled by people just like you and me who desire to speak their minds. We are fortunate to live in a country that hands it to us as a birthright. No country nor system is perfect, however, and over the years, those who believed that their due freedom was held back from them, spoke up. It's not magic that creates movements and marches. It's the individuals who opened their mouths.

Standing alone, speaking up, gives us strength – the backbone that makes a man or a woman. It means taking that big gulp of air and paying no heed to your sweaty palms and speaking your mind and heart, regardless of the consequences. Sometimes, we may not feel so titanic when we speak up. It may shrivel our innards and we may want to take back what took us so long to get out. Even though our voice may have sounded shaky, it's the meaning behind the words and the willingness to speak that count. In our country, Freedom is available. It's up to us to use it, and speak up when we need to. It's our right, our liberty, and, most important, our choice.

These winning photographs taken by 100 PARADE readers are chronicles of Freedom. Each photo pinpoints a moment or a mood that reflects upon the theme of Freedom and its gifts. Freedom is the lineup of colorful newspaper dispensers in front of a government building in Washington, D.C. Or, it can be found in the budding patriotism of a group of students who threaded red, white and blue tissues in a school fence to create a flag – the icon of our Freedom.

Freedom can be lonely, but it's the triumphant and spirited sounds that it makes when we speak up together, on our own, to create the mighty music. With an unleashed fervor, freedom sings.

Every American is
guaranteed the freedoms in the U.S. Bill of Rights, but we may not always be aware of them.
And many of us tend to take them for granted. However, if we feel our freedoms have been
denied, we will fight for them. As a talk show host I've heard many accounts of the injustices
suffered by some American citizens. And there are people who have been denied
their constitutional rights.

On TV, we tackle many of these issues. I actually thought it would be easy to depict
something so profoundly American in a photograph. Then I tried to think of one image to convey
the idea of freedom and it suddenly became very difficult. Why? Because freedom is a concept
and it's not tangible. You can't wrap it up and give it to your friend for his birthday. It has too many
forms: freedom of religion, of choice, to bear arms.

The struggle for these freedoms in our history is what makes our country different.
It's the foundation of our society and our most precious commodity.
Luckily for the judges of the PARADE-Kodak "Let Freedom Ring" photography contest,
there are many symbols that have become synonymous with this concept over
the past 200 years.

As you turn the pages of this book, you'll see the bald eagle, the American Flag and the Statue
of Liberty. You'll also see some very different and creative interpretations of what
freedom means to the individual. Take a look at the "Living Flag," or Allen Ray Lamont of the
Oglala Sioux celebrating his native culture.

Judging this contest was a great experience. It opened my eyes and made me think what a unique
society we live in. These photographs are both a tribute to we the people of the United States and a
happy celebration of the 200th Anniversary of the Bill of Rights.